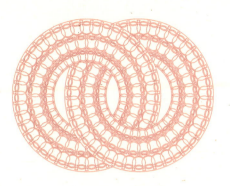

The Body at a Loss

The Body at a Loss

Cati Porter

CAVANKERRY
PRESS

CavanKerry Press Ltd.
Fort Lee, New Jersey
www.cavankerrypress.org

Publisher's Cataloging-In-Publication Data
(Prepared by The Donohue Group, Inc.)
Names: Porter, Cati, author.
Title: The body at a loss / Cati Porter.
Other Titles: Laurel books.
Description: First edition. | Fort Lee, New Jersey : CavanKerry Press, 2019.
Identifiers: ISBN 9781933880716
Subjects: LCSH: Porter, Cati—Health—Poetry. | Breast—Cancer—Psychological aspects—Poetry. | Breast—Cancer—Treatment—Poetry. | Mothers and daughters—Poetry.
Classification: LCC PS3616.O76 B64 2019 | DDC 811/.6—dc23

Book design and typesetting by Mayfly Design
First Edition 2019, Printed in the United States of America

The Body at a Loss is the 15th title of CavanKerry's Literature of Illness imprint. LaurelBooks are fine collections of poetry and prose that explore the many poignant issues associated with confronting serious physical and/or psychological illness.

CavanKerry Press is grateful for the support it receives from the New Jersey State Council on the Arts.

ALSO BY CATI PORTER

small fruit songs (2008)

Seven Floors Up (2008)

(al)most delicious (2010)

what Desire makes of us (2011, 2015)

The Way Things Move The Dark (2013)

My Skies of Small Horses (2016)

The Body, Like Bread (2016)

For my mothers. And in memory of my friend.

Contents

IV. The Blue-Mouthed Blossom Descends

V. Cast the Net, the Moment Slips Cleanly

I am terrified by this dark thing
That sleeps in me;
All day I feel its soft, feathery turnings, its malignity.

—SYLVIA PLATH, FROM "ELM"

Administering My Dog's Cancer Therapy, I Think about My Sons

My thumb and forefinger pinch a pill as I thrust my fist
        back into his throat. His teeth, a bracelet
        of blunt tines, rake gently across my wrist.
        I pull out my hand, sticky with saliva,
        and hold his mouth closed
        and stroke his neck
        until I am certain he has swallowed.

At seven years old he is two years older than
        my oldest son. He is my oldest son,
        I tell myself, but of course, he is not.
        He is just the dog, I remind myself daily,
        because, if he were my son,
        I would okay the endoscopy, biopsy
        the lining of his stomach. I would make the drive
        into the next county for intravenous chemotherapy.

Once he ate reluctantly from my hand chicken breasts
        boiled for him on my stove. If he were
        my son, I would not hand-feed him
        the breasts of dead chickens. I would slice
        off my own, boil them
        pink to white in my very best pot.
        I would shred them, feed them to him
        warm, if only to keep him through the night.

I.

The Meadow and the Distant Calling

When My Mother Finds a Lump in Her Breast,

It is like finding one in my own.

"Mom's Surgery Instructions"

—A Found Poem

MAY 31

Between 9 & 11 or 2 & 4:30,
        no appointment,
no fasting

Second floor check in
        (same place you went
for the appointment with Doctor Zekos)

JUNE 7—SURGERY

8:15 a.m. Breast Imaging,
        behind hospital, on Brockton,
For "wire locator"   (?)

THEN go
        to Riverside Community Hospital
Check in at noon
        for "injection of dye"

Surgery at 2:30
        Outpatient!
Released the same day

QUESTIONS TO ASK:

If they determine during surgery
        that they see more cancer,
                will they just take more?

What if they determine
      during the lumpectomy
            that it would be better
      to just take the whole breast? Will they
do that on the spot or wait for a second surgery?

Before the surgery,
      do you need to fast?
When should you stop the Plavix?

How long will the lumpectomy take,
      and what time should you expect
            to be released to go home?

Turning the Line

In the mirror I examine the line, the indent,
    The implied narrative, withheld,
And in the poem, I examine the way the turning
    Of the line implies a body's inscriptions:
How prescriptive, this instance of making
    One well through the medicine of poetry, &
The pills, and how to render them within
    The water round on the palate,
        The button of the pill on
            The tongue, the scratch,
    The pill catching in the throat;
    The ease with which this all takes place

How the body must know itself, and yet
    The mind knows less—
Knows how to hold a glass, how to bring
    Water to the lips, how tender
But once inside, the body takes it in, takes over,
    And the mind can do no more
Than provide entry. How invisible,
    Immutable, these inner workings
How as the body turns on itself, as the mind turns
    Inward to examine the cause—

How the story unfolds
    How the map leads nowhere
        How the roads are all languorous and cool and unpaved
    How the dust thrown obscures the landscape
How the mirror is a sham, an inversion, never true
    How the indent and the line remain even
        As you train them to follow another course

Nocturne

Some nights I dream of gasoline, of flames, of
Running barefoot through sprinklers in the dark in my
Night dress, late as always, slipping stupidly
On the damp lawn, sprawled cold beneath
The streetlamp's yellow flare

Others, I dream of a towering city, skyscrapers
The car whooshes between and over, skimming
The rooftops as blue lava erupts, as buildings collapse
Into ruin as the driver and I dodge the flow, dart
Between blue hot fountains, shelter
In a dim apartment as we wait for the fall

Other nights, I dream of faceless women
With my name, of a gaping house, a shifting
Feast laid out on tables amid a skittering crowd.
We move between rooms, feigning estrangement.
These dreams pile up, indecipherable,
Notes taken in a handwriting that I recognize
As my own, but cannot comprehend

Initiation

Because I have complained,
Now the doctor can feel a mass

In my neck
And I am referred to

The sonograph technician
Who presses her device deep

Into the soft tissue,
Edging each clavicle.

A smattering like night stars,
Many grainy moons

On the monitor:
Nodules bob amid

Red and blue splotches
Denoting temperature, blood flow.

I can see my carotid arteries
Throbbing, see myself

As if viewing a distant new galaxy.
Pulsing, embryonic, gestating,

As it was in that long moment
When my belly housed a child,

That familiar chill as I tried to interpret
The blurry image on the sonogram

The way one gazes into tea leaves for answers
To questions you don't yet know you have.

Reading Miller's Essay "On Tragedy and the Common Man" with My Teenage Son the Night before Receiving the Radiologist's Report

My teenage son struggles to interpret Miller's prose
Which to me says nothing more than
We're all in this together, that tragedy
Is not a state reserved for nobility
But instead can afflict us all.
So when my son asks me to help with his essay,
I happily oblige, because: how much
Longer do I have with him, really?

And when Miller cites the psychology
Of Oedipus and Orestes, I ask and am informed
That my son neither wants to marry me, nor to kill me;
Instead, he just wants to finish the damn essay.
So I struggle to translate Miller's turns of phrase
Into language my son can understand: mocking jays,
And the strategy of applying one's intellect
To save one's skin. The drama of loss.

When the structure of the essay requires him
To choose sides—either with or against Miller—
He opts to remain unconvinced, although
I suspect that if I had done a better job
He would be more willing to risk being wrong.

In the morning I will pick up the radiologist's report
Which will tell me at which particular crossroads
I stand, but what good does it do us to fixate
On endings when everything depends
Upon the liminal, the little deaths that happen each day
While we wait to live.

Taking My Time

Woke up to the sound of rain. Two eggs on toast
And a cup of coffee, a cat napping
On the news. In my robe on a Tuesday morning,
The sound of the rain like typing on the lawn.

The coughing starts early today, each hitch,
Each hiccup, a jolt. In an hour I will be in the office
Of my GP, going over the radiology results.
But for now, I can imagine the outcome

Any way I like. Sunny side up. Early sounds
Of traffic whir, tires splashing up oily waves
At the curb. I can still pretend that I have not already
Read the report. If I sit still and quiet, the coughing

Subsides. If I drink the coffee, slowly. If I take care
Not to wake the children. In the kitchen, the dishes
In a tipsy pile, each plate uncertain, like each day.

What Lies Between

—For Buzz and for Violet

A song comes on the radio and inexplicably
I cry while driving, my voice too hoarse
To sing along, each failed note calling up
A cough, each taken breath sharp in my throat
Like breathing smog, the breath in my body
Like water in a too-shallow bath—not quite enough
To submerge, but enough to bathe.

I recall a photo of my friend's father
Bent into a backwards L,
Leaning to shimmy beneath a lowering stick.
Life is like that, the stick lowering ever lower,
Our backs like matchsticks bent back,
Our flaming heads burning, burning, done;
The lights dim to a cooler hue, flicker, falter, fail.
I think of my friend's father now,
Frail hands grasping the bar of his walker,
His nine decades whittling him thin. I think
Of my father's mother, her cool cool hands,
Reaching for the names of things that escape her.
I buckle her seatbelt, serve her only soft foods.

When I was small, I would arc the swing
So that my feet were in relief against the sky,
And upside-down the world. Or climbing,
I would lick the bars, the cool sharp tang
Of curved metal against my tongue. Once
I did a cherry drop, not content to let the other girls
Best me. I monkey-swung across to the middle,
Doubled up my legs, knees caught upon the rungs,
Torso hung beneath, then slipped chin-first

Into sand. The blood was more than I had
Ever seen, holding an icepack to my wound
Over the bathroom sink, the flap of skin
Coated in scratchy grains like bread crumbs.
On the drive to the emergency room,
The school principal's wife and my teacher
Kept looking over their shoulder at me
In the back seat, and then came to a stop
So quickly that my head hit the seat back, rebounding.
I can still feel the dull ache of the anesthetist's needle,
Recall the stitches, the thread's taut pull through flesh.

Yesterday my teenage son cursed me
For tearing down the rotted backyard swing set.
I've destroyed his childhood. He will never
Get it back. I will never get it back, nor my own.
I remind him we still have photographs and memories
But that's not enough.

My grandmother shows me
A photo of herself at sixteen, dark hair and red lips, just married.
What did she know of the hard years ahead,
The philandering but loving husband, the other
Who would run a man down while drunk,
The piles of money he would call her to retrieve
Upon arrest, salvaged from the abandoned car
After a night at the tables; the baby in her belly
Who would birth her own at fourteen, or me,
Daughter of her middle child, second son.
What does she remember.

I want to attribute
My lost voice to something ordinary, my crying
To the sudden swing of chemicals causing
My body's ablations, blood and cells sloughed off,
And not to errant cells run amuck, the body's

Silent rebellion. And suddenly all I want is to linger
In the bath, aching and bloody as I am, red blooming
Out like clouds. I am reminded that there are no guarantees.

All that I am is what I am now, and now, and now.

Fork

Prongs point to
A variance where
There are multiple
Ways this could
Go and you are
Standing on a shifting
Platform shoes
Don't protect
Your feet they know
The way to the edge
Of the woods
Where there is
A signal flare
Rising up from
The meadow
And the distant
Calling of geese
On the lake there
A pontoon bobbing
Along the wake
Of a passing skiff
Motoring past
The moored shore
And the fork is more
A series of options
Signaling direction
All signs obliterated
By the glare.

II.

Shoes
Skimming
the
Ocean
Floor

By the Sound of It

On mute, the television displays closed-captioned words
As the mouths of a man and a woman wince open and shut,
Teeth clicking silently as the sounds of things are translated.

Onscreen, the words *paper tears*—
                          And then the woman's tears
Like paper streamers drip from the corners of her eyes, cross
The Mojave of her cheeks, unfurl like banners off the precipice

Of her chin. At her feet they pool in curls until she is ankle-deep
In a paper puddle, paper tide pool, paper waves lapping.
She climbs atop the kitchen table, now afloat, and drifts

Through the corridors, watching as rooms are subsumed by flood.
Grabbing a floor lamp, she pushes off as the latent electricity disperses
As power meets water, uses the lamp as a makeshift oar,

Unlatches the front door, and a river transforms the street.
A great paper storm is roaring through. The neighbor's dog,
Atop his drifting Dogloo, mouths an incessant unspooling

Of letters: *aroof aroof—aroof aroof—aroof aroof—aroof aroof aroof—*

Beside me, my husband shifts, and without a sound, moves
My hand to rub his aching head, moves his head to accommodate
The shape of my hand, his own armed with the remote, aimed

At the screen—
                As the button is pressed, I glimpse a man in a suit
Straddling a desk, paddling after the woman, paper waves now cresting,
The tide rising, the dog and the man both gazing at the sky, their eyes
Seeming to scan the distance, wondering, *Who will save us now?*

The Present, Tense

I am walking in the field and this is
All there is; all there ever is, is this:

Mornings like a broken yolk in the pan,
Midday rye with mayo and tomato,

The late afternoon gold flakes of shirred leaves
Riffled by the breeze, dogs barking at squirrels,

Each other. Sad coyotes at dusk trot
Their dun bodies into the lit field, find

A catch to gnash their teeth against. Nights
The field becomes a natty blue bedspread

As you dream the sky is a blackboard, each
Chalky name a star erasing slowly.

Which do you remember, do you forget?
And what if there is no field? Only this

Misremembering. And the field does change
The field does turn, thin green shoots filling in,

Shoots that erupt into soft heads that fall
Then hurry the thorned balls that catch on socks,

Infiltrate the lip of your sneakers, rage
Against bony ankles. Winters whitewash

The details, gray the animal bodies
That make their way across this forever unfolding field.

We Set Sail for the Margins

Because we cannot tolerate
Getting to the heart of it
We instead skirt
      the edges,
           a pencil
      not maxi,
      not A-line;
           hits
           at the knees.

Not tweed,
      not fabric, not at all,
      not that you noticed.
I can barely walk shoes skimming
           the ocean floor.

The issue is not what to wear,
      but what not to talk about.
      You don't know
           what to say; skirt it—

Meanwhile,
      the urchins ask
What there is to eat,
      and I say,
           Eat what you like.
           There are no further questions.

Since You Insist

I do not resist   easily.   Facts
conspire, and yes,   my respiration *is*
a little sketchy.   You say the truth
can only be told   in fiction, but I say
the truth can also   be told in a vacuum,
shouting down the length,   a lens at both ends.
Seeing is as seeing does,   which is to say,
everything and nothing   is open to interpretation.
I would write it all down   but the facts keep shifting,
the truth a moving target.   When I say *run*, you better
know that I mean,   *please stay*. When I say, *please stay,*
you better know   that I mean really, *please don't, go.*

Even at Their Best, Doctors Only Guess

One says its nothing, another says it might not be.
Even the radiologist who biopsies my neck
Views the results suspiciously;

Even after the ultrasound, snow on the monitor,
Each nodule and hunk of flesh explored
Via the smooth arc of the roving probe,

No one knows for sure until the surgeon
Peels back skin, removes the foreign object
That really is not that foreign, is you, or was, a part of—

But in the interim: tests.

For Your Amusement

We enter the white-coated room:
I, in my gown: not beaded, not embroidered

The machine surrounds, the railing on the ceiling
Moves parts into position

And I, on my feet
Before a vertical table,
Tilt back
Toward the floor

Hold on.

And now I am flat
And now I am a corkscrew on a board
And now I am a log doing a roll

Drink this, they say, and I do
Silly me

White mustachioed
Mouth full of chalk

Resonant Images

On my back in the white tunnel, the jackhammers
& pile drivers pound the silence. My mind finds
Meaning in the clatter as I drift between states,
Dreaming it is over, that I am everyman, anyone.

I don't believe you, but the stirring is confusing
In this white state, floating on a raft of thought.
Nice to see you. I believe I know you.

What freeway is that, what distant flyover
That I levitate toward, you steering beside me,
One hand on the wheel, one hand in my lap, spinning
Me out toward an ecstatic turn?

The Solution

One day you awaken to the sound of waves
    And the world has dissolved, as sugar into water—

The sudden shift in being, from solid into liquid,
    And your matter no longer matters, and when you rise up

To the surface you find there is no surface,
    That all potential universes have in fact melted

Into each other, and that all that could be
    Had, said, done, been, true,

Has melded into one, fluid as the sea,
    Empty and full at once—because that is the way

Of it, as one day the world seems steady, solid, then
    The next, the world is nothing more than a vast unboundedness

Where we drift with currents that are driven
    By no moon, no you.

III.

Orchestral

Blood

and

Bone

Small Knots

The harder I pull, the tighter the knot.
My son's shoe in my lap, my nail picks at it like lice.
Untangle the mess, untangle the thought.

Morning tangles with night in the brightening pot.
Sip coffee—no sugar, no cream, just ice.
The harder I pull, the tighter the knot.

Two children, two cats, a house bought.
Two decades, and all that will suffice.
Untangle the mess, untangle the thought.

The weeks weave links into a chain time wrought.
Necklace in the box long-lost, double-knotted. Twice.
The harder I pull, the tighter the knot,

But loosen it, and suddenly the nail pricks free, unclots
The laces, tongue freed from its vise.
Untangle the mess, untangle the thought.

The job done, morning is shot,
The coffee is cold, and my nightclothes offer bad advice.
The harder I pull, the tighter the knot.
Untangle the mess, untangle the thought.

My Mother's Breasts

After the final exam
Before the lumpectomy,
From behind
An imperfectly
Drawn curtain
I glimpse
In the mirror
As my mother
With her back
To me trades
The flimsy pastel gown
For her Maidenform bra
My own breasts,
Distorted by years
That I have not
Yet accumulated.

Incidental

In the womb
      of the throat,
            an incubation
                  embedded
     cry, baby
         I rock the body
              to sleep & we sleep

I wake
     & it wakes
         but can't speak
            nipple-locked,
    a form of suckling

The body
     inviolate, invaded, inflates

Conditions ripe for growth
     I don't know
         that it's there
     but I do

Sweet thing,
     I must not
Feed you

Match

Show me the water, I will show you the milk.
We pair up and break down, upending.

The bridge is made of bread, greening & sinking.
The fruit floats, little berries head-bobbing.

My mouth in the water.
My mouth angling for the berry.

Nothing sustains us,
Nothing as a substitute for air, for silence,

Silence the filling in of all that aches,
All that bobs in the water, lobbed to shore.

I am the bread, the milk.
I am the house on the edge, crumbling.

The birds have a habit of (not) helping.
I am the river, the birds.

Souring & blueing, the thick milk curdling.
I can't feed you the way I can

The feckless fox, the calculating rabbit.
I take your head, which is my own,

In my hands, in my lap: the house stills.
I massage the sand from between your ears,

Wrong as the shallow waters that swallow
The young, the sweet-breathed milk-eaters that saw.

How we abandon ourselves to the wolves.
How we are ourselves the wolves.

I am the match, I am flammable.
God damn it all if I don't burn it down.

Tear

I want to rip my own throat out,
Nails digging into skin, confettied flesh
Curling out from beneath the tips
But I cannot bring myself
To break through that flimsy barrier
Between the butterfly aching out,
The outside aching in.

How my own hands betray me,
My words, clipped wings, battering.
The orchestral blood and bone
And muscle and tendon,
That play themselves out
As though their song were the answer.

I want to rip words from my throat
And fling them, hard words,
Hoarded, words that brick my tongue
Into the mouth of the cave. A cough
And the sounds echo and tumble.
Climb lower into the trunk of the body,
Lower the lid to keep out the light.

My Mother's Hats

When my friend Marion, my mother's age,
First was diagnosed, she went with her hairdresser, Joey,
To "Wigs on Wheels" to select, while she still could,
A replacement coif that most closely
Matched her own hair.

Not my mother.

Even as it thinned, even when down to baby fuzz,
Still no wig, though we did peruse the catalogs.
After chemo. After radiation. Her solution
Became an array of berets, cloche,
Newsboys, straw, knit.

IV.

The

Blue-Mouthed

Blossom

Descends

Surgical Precision

It doesn't hurt
That I can see

That the surgeon
Has such small

Beautiful hands,
Tender in the way

They extend
From the wrist

To smooth
A shoulder,

Their firm, calm
Pressure.

The Boundaries of the Body

I don't believe in the afterlife, but when

The nurses escort me to the amber-lit room

And I am laid gently down on a featherbed

Surrounded by these angels, I hear

The chirruping of ladies-in-waiting

Commingling with the nearby pained wails

Of saints, and come to believe I may have arrived.

A kiss on my hand needle-sharp &

A pale tape to keep it secure,

Displacement through careful placement,

The cool coil leashing me to the bed.

Nothing beneath, the crushed lavender

Paper gown, my body a confusion

Of hands smoothing, this stupor.

When the feathery schooner is set adrift

Down the interminably white breezy hall,

The widening doors swing open on command &

I feel as if I am moving between, that is,

As though I am gliding.

A large metal-framed wheeled cart blocking our path

An obstacle to collapse through

As we make our way.

In the anteroom the recessed lights

Glare, but in the theater they are as hospitable as

White honeycombs that loom overhead

On stems that glow and gloss the bluing figures,

Flowering faces masked, and hands

A slow flurry of connecting and disconnecting.

Here the minute clicks open

Like a coin purse, the seconds spilling

Lean as I gather my attention

Into a tight knot, a bud, a fist, welled breaths

That pin me to a center that anchors all others

Spread about like jostled corn,

Like a coin of grain loosened for the geese.

The blue-mouthed blossom descends

And the crisp apple of oxygen fills me as I float

And the balloon world

Expands as it contracts.

~

When I awaken, a clear coiled tube
Smooth & wound beneath my palm.

Pain muffled like sharp cheddar
Between slices of brown bread heavy

As my body against the mattress, weighted
As something I so want that I cannot.

The stiff clinking of voices, glassy
Recollection of dreaming—but what?—

And then the dim light of going home.
Disrobing, the lavender paper petal-thin

And failing, my body an unarticulated sound,
My head attached by a dim stripe of tape

Bobs atop my neck, flowerhead, deadheaded.
The wheedling chair going clickety-clickety.

Crackling in my head like a paperweight dropped
To the curb, the discordant shards contained

Behind the globe's smooth skin. Lifted
To the seat, the dank sea foam of asphalt rising up

To greet the tires as they roll toward home.
My throat a thick band of disbelief, the letters of words

Catching like ice chips, melting back, rejoining the floe.

૨&

The white lozenges click into place

And the pain dissolves like chalk into water,

Coating my insides cleanly in a thin

Imperceptible wash. So when the night

Through the body ticks and tumbles,

Broken-chain-link loose,

The head a wire brush

Gooped by the slow sinking

Into quicksand, the quick rise

Of each short doughy breath

Two steps forward one step

Forward ever forward, and like

A barge on water each crest lifts

As the vials flatten into eddies

That intrigue, the small shelf

That catches me squarely as I drift,

Levels me, a bubble's arc on repeat,

As I lie suspended like a dropped chain

Stitch, like needles clicking, the night

Drawling itself out of a nest of yarn.

And out of that nightful ocean
An immense glacier islands up
Through crepuscular fog &

Suddenly I am pinned and searing,
Skin to ice, unpeeling, white-visored,
Leaden with pain, the red wailing.

And now rough hands clip me in,
Interrogate the silence, and the glacial
Breaks with the turbulent wheels.

And all my eyes can find to fixate on
Are the obstetrical kits in the overhead bin
Bound in place with a plastic tie.

And the body remembers
What it was like to berth a body,
To cut a body free.

I am returning to the soapstone
Center of the fruit, soft flesh
Falling all around me.

Nerve and bone, clipped wires,
Voice and hands irrationally silent.
I want nothing but the noise of a needle

Breaking skin, the shattering flush
Of cool liquid breaching, and absent
That, want nothing

But the wading into the river,
Pockets full.

ठ⃝

The voices turn and return

On repeat, not sing-song, not

Soothing. This levitating body

Is not mine. I am told it is time

To take it home. In the hours

That follow sleep is a dog

That circles and circles, my rough

Hand licked smooth by its papery tongue,

My pillowing body never quite enough.

It is the underworld that draws me, the slipping between

The here and the here, the not quite, and in this

Is a hollow place where my body fits,

A puzzle box that rattles when shaken.

When the berg melts my body is a puddle

And my mind at its center recalls

The angels it knows it does not know.

The emergence of a clear thought.

A series of clear thoughts.

A series of moments strung together,

Bright bulbs glittering on the line.

The Body at a Loss

I don't know how it has to come to this—
The slit throat, the unguent wound.

Yes, I do know. I know how the body
Turns, the traitorous rising up

Of the lymphocytic swarms, the swell
Crowd rushing the site like an ambush,

The body's defenses defending against
Itself, itself the enemy. How like the body

To make of itself its own battlefield,
Its own armies both agonist and protagonist

In the autobiography of cellular decay.
So like the child who rises up against

The imposed rules, written in the interest
Of the child, for the preservation of the child;

So like the fragile peace earned through
Chemical intervention, complacency

A byproduct of the reduced momentum
Enforced by the constant bombardment

Of neutral territory with a wash of hormones
That confuse the issue. I apply a salve to the wound,

Wait for it to heal, the inability to look left
Or right completely, the head atop the neck,

The neck the stem, the hollow in the throat
Where the spoon carved out its own reflection

Until the body cried *no more*, and the throat
Closed, and the war was over, or was it?

The Body as the Object of Affection

1.

I want to love the body that loves me back,
My hands finding the groove, the smooth
Curve, the alley, the hallway, the foyer,
The belly as topographical map, hands that need
No direction, lost as they are

Self-conscious, my hand traces
The curling edges of the bandage,
Finds the seam, considers the options

How many times have you done this
How to disclose the wound
I want you to love the object as it was meant to be loved

She says she undresses for you
The stars shine through
The holes, pinpricks in the sky of her

2.

You find an opening, an entrance,
My body wide with hope, the hollow
Throat, the words having abandoned

I want you inside me but you are already
I want my mouth around you,
But you are my mouth;
You are my teeth, you are my breasts,
You are my breath, so close, we drift
Into the amniotic ocean, salted skin
Afloat, my hair tangled with the kelp,
Our hands tangled together

Lace your fingers with my own,
Now lace them with hers, with his, with ours,
So many hands; kiss me,
If only to begin again

At First

It is light when she is discharged
And she is aloft on narcotics,
Awakened as from a dream
To now occupy the passenger seat

Her husband holds her hand
While they drive
She is warm
The day could not possibly
Be more beautiful

The setting sun
The road smooth,
Untraveled

A dark ribbon running
Beneath the tires
As they pass the amusement park
With its dull rides
And bright riders
And somewhere within
Someone is surely kissing

Home, and she is led
Into the bedroom
Where the sugar of down
And flannel invite her
Into the French film she watches
Through late evening

She wants to love there
And the warm red soup in the ceramic mug
Has never tasted so wonderful, like velvet
The throbbing at the incision site
Recedes until it is just an itch
That can't be scratched

So lovely, the bed and the lilting voices

In the Cabin-Dark Bedroom

The only observable light
Is a cracked door down the hall

The destabilized body
Offset by the head that fills
With a heavy liquor
And depresses the pillow
Rejects the angle
So the husband
Moves the pillow
The body now
Lying flat rejects
That flatness until
Pillows are stacked
Torso raised
Ice packs melt
Glacially down the forehead,
Warm to an irritating berm
At the base of the neck
Where the ache between
Skull and shoulder
Blades deepens

The head an olive
The teeth of the pain
Grind through, meet
The pit of skull,
The mind a kindness
That the body withholds

The top of the head
Presses up to the ceiling

The exquisite pressure builds
As the ceiling bears down

Tongue a pill and water
And it all comes back,
Body raised and retching
Red soup as sirens arrive

The emergence of technicians
Who take the elbow
And guide the body
To the gurney, all bed rails
Spongy surface, a lip
That catches at the hatch
Of the vehicle, legs that
Collapse as the bed is slid
Into the hull, the lurching
Down the highway,
The highway's ridges erupting
Up through the undercarriage
Into the body that lies
Still to quell the pain

The mind cannot
Find a foothold, cannot
Grasp even
The rough edges

The rapid thunk
Of wheeled legs unfolding
Beneath and the crush of asphalt

Double doors—double nurses
Chatting because it is just another
Emergency & who is this numb woman
Who can barely croak her name

Here a warm blanket
Tossed folded at the foot of the bed
Where the woman's hands
Cannot travel cannot dislodge

From the posture while
The nurse continues to
Repeat the question

The cheerful whiteboard
With nurse names and smileys

The forever-later pleasant doctor
Who again repeats the question

Until the final cool relief via a tube in the hand
And she is a creature in an ocean guided
By a fluorescent moon rafting and rising and falling
Toward home

This

He holds her hand as she steadies herself
To disrobe, turns the shower spigot
To warm, warmer, holds her hand
As she steps in, sits on the stool
Beneath the spray

Lifting hands above her head
Causes a deep deep ache

She cannot tip her head back toward the spray

He waits while she smoothes the suds
With loofah up and down her unshaven legs,
Her arms, across her back, her hair beading,
The delicious heat, and he holds her
Hand as she steps out dripping,

And now he wrings the water from her hair,
Dabs the wet bandage, brushes her hair

This braided life, this tangled, aching bliss

The Fly Implores You to Attend to Your Life

How many days have I gone unseen, your back
To me as I perched the encumbered stacks
Of papers, my slight weight too light to shift
The pile, or hovering, reading over your shoulder.
What lies you tell yourself to live by, that a life
Spent seeking meaning makes up for the life
Less-lived. But I have only the short wisdom of a fly.
I whisper truth into your ear; you bat me away.
What can a fly say anyway, what use, words,
When all you hear is what catches, and what's heard
Often is not what was said. And so I fear
The only lesson I have left for you is to sear,
Stubborn feet to the light, so that death may feel
As near as your breath, less one turn of the wheel.

V. Cast the Net, the Moment Slips Cleanly

Aubade

Last night the wind woke the chimes
While I and the children slept,
While you pressed the wax deeper
Into your ear, and the muffled
Night-sounds filtered in as through
A sieve, sifting out the sediment.

How many nights have we slept
Like this—you, bundled into
Your solitude, and I, amidst
The bustling of kids and cats,
Of the gate clanging open.

Nights like this we dream
Our separate dreams, the hours
Dissipating, familiar as steam.

Wake, Butterfly, It's Late

Bat lashes together
So close I can taste your breath

In the pool, fly, arms
Motoring toward the deep end

In a back pocket,
A knife, for safekeeping

Examine all the ways—
On a plate, the filet flayed

In the gravel on the trail,
A ragged monarch, splayed

In the body, in the hollow
Of the clavicle, an unfolding

An organ playing
Its heavy music

Lengthening
Into the one long note

Then, gone

Epiphany in the Shower

How else, indeed, to clap the net over the butterfly of the moment?

—VITA SACKVILLE-WEST

1.

Hold it in my hand, prickly as a fish.
It undulates between cupped palms,
The river at my feet catching it as it falls

2.

Back to the spray, I bend
Toward dropped
Soap, green
Shifting as whorls
Of water raft it
Anywhere but where
I need it to be

3.

Caught by currents, I have already
Moved away from the precarious rocks,
Already cannot remember what it felt like
To approach them, to not know
Whether the raft would crash
Upon or dodge them, have already
Forgotten the rush & relief
That comes from knowing that
The danger has passed

4.

Cast the net, the moment slips
Cleanly through
Nothing exists but this,
Yet even as I write
I forget what it is
That I mean to say

False / Alarm

We are gathered together in the lobby
of an Embassy Suites
when my stepmom gives us the news:
Six months or so, then she will be gone.

That was more than a decade ago
and she's still here. Two decades past
her breast sliced cleanly off, the pink pucker
of a diagonal scar the only remnants,
and three past the last melanoma scare.

Her kidney gone rogue, cells took up
residence in her lungs, her spleen,
now gone, part of her kidney, gone.
She is still here, but each new scan
a fresh start to the death stare.

How many addendums can we write into
our own obituaries?

Dear Teo, with the abdominal tumor
the size of a grapefruit. Dear Ann Jo,
whose cancer fizzed her brain like Pop Rocks.
Dear Lucy. Dear Devin. Dear Marion.

Tiny Baby Cancer,

The doctor says; *micropapillary carcinoma*,
My chart reads—and I am made aware

Of the pinprick that was not the canary
But the gummy swallowtail extracted.

The disruption was nothing, after all, and in fact
These months later the cough is still there,

And I now know that so much of what
Aggrieves us is of our own doing.

And when the blood test reveals the tumor
Marker as *possible* (but not probable) evidence

That all illness has not been vanquished,
It is both vindication and salutatory gesture

Toward a life not fully lived. Still learning
How to mitigate any potential disaster; how to view it

Without distortion; how to live fully acknowledging
There is always a diagnosis, and not always a cure.

Marion & My Mother

At the cancer center, they bond over Lebed & potlucks.
Pronounced "clean," their hair returns.
Their nails thicken and harden.

My mother's port is removed—that hole in her chest
Protected by a plastic cap where the chemo was fed.
Marion's is removed too.
The world resumes its predictable spin.

I see Marion the day that she gets the call,
And the world is off-balance again
As she learns that the cancer has returned
To burn through organ and bone.

During the last weeks, I sit with my friend
Who slowly descends into that place
No one can return from, hold her hand and listen
As she rocks forward and back,
As the intolerable twitching in her limbs
Begins to subside, replaced by an expression
That denotes the final terrible inward spiral.

I think of Marion's daughter, en route for a final visit.
She is somewhere in Central California
When she gets the call, half-way between
Home and *home,* while I get to go home to my own mother,

Who is waiting, always, to tell me something.
Today I have something to tell her too.

An Inconvenient Year

—For Marion Mitchell-Wilson, 1946–2015

At the memorial, the hall is lined with chairs, two hundred
Bodies pressed close, the August air thick with their perfume.

In my hand, the glossy program laced with images:
Marion as a young woman, mother, later.

Her college roommate sings "The Way We Were"
And I think of my mother beside me, her own

Diagnosis, treatment, and remission; Marion's
Fat binder labeled "An Inconvenient Year"

On loan as we fumbled through the same series
Of diagnostics, chemo, & radiation,

At a time when Marion's own treatments
Had been pronounced *done*.

My mother's hats now sit stacked on the table, for donation.
Her hair is back. The cancer is . . . gone?

Marion is gone. On the patio, I take a slug
Of champagne, another, and again.

She would have scoffed at me crying—
Sweetie, no tears.

Her daughter at the podium spoke
Of her as a woman who knew precisely what she wanted,

Even until the end; someone always up for a night cap;
A splash of something spicy in the glass.

Kentucky bourbon, straight. "Rebel Yell."
I'll take a glass of that.

Patient Survey

In the waiting room, a glowing fish tank
Emanates from a flat screen hung high above
Our heads. The goldfish flit, the bubbles gurgle,
And the pump swooshes pixelated water
Through a pixelated filter & back
Into the goldfish hush.

On the walkway toward the Wellness Center's
Door, I take care to avoid crushing the snails.
What separates *them* from *us*? How patiently they
Make their way from one piece of grass to
Another, dragging their glittering trains. I lift one,
Move it to the other side. But who am I to know
Where it was headed? Suppose I have just set it
In a patch of salt, imminent death?

What is it that plucks us from the rush
Deposits us this side or that side; what care
Have they taken to avoid us smashing into the dust?

On the end table a stack of pamphlets,
Patient Survey. How patient they are, waiting,
The stack fanned out as though many hands
Might reach for them at once.

Where It Begins

It begins, again, with pancakes. Or rather
it begins with the question of pancakes,
of whether or not they will have ears.
No, it begins like this: me in my robe
at the kitchen table with coffee,
cell phone at my ear, looking out
through dirty glass, listening
to my work-bound husband.
No, it begins with the one-eyed
mother cat, languid on the brittle lawn.
No, it begins with her two orange kittens
draped across her skinny belly. No,
it begins with peeling my husband's
boiled eggs, with pouring his coffee
into a travel mug. It begins with seeing
him out the door, with a quick kiss. No,
it begins with waking up in our child's bed,
with falling asleep the night before
with our child who could not fall asleep—no,
not the youngest, the oldest, heavy
in the upper bunk, awake and alone in the dark,
in his wakefulness. Actually, it begins
with a shared beer, a nodding off on the couch,
the trek down the hall, & children with
raucous toothbrush songs. No, it begins
with the feeding of the inside cats, with
outside cats looking in, kittens keening
at the window, little kitten ears like funnels
taking it all in. No. It doesn't begin here.
There is a sudden sound of something
opening. A pop, a fizzle. A nuzzle. Soon
there are pancakes: some with ears, some
without. The day is about to start.

There is a moon and stars on the griddle:
a constellation of wants,
a universe of new beginnings.

Acknowledgments

Hartskill Review: "Patient Survey"

MockingHeart Review: "Match," "The Fly Implores You to Attend to Your Life",
    "Wake, Butterfly, It's Late"

PoetryMagazine.com: "We Set Sail for the Margins," "Since You Insist"

West Trestle: "Reading Miller's Essay 'On Tragedy and the Common Man' with
    My Teenage Son the Night before Receiving the Radiologist's Report"

White Ink: Poems on Mothers and Motherhood: "Administering My Dog's
    Cancer Therapy, I Think about My Sons"

Writer's Digest Poetic Asides blog: "Taking My Time," top ten finalist, day 1,
    Robert Lee Brewer's 2014 NaPoWriMo poem-a-day challenge

Nothing is ever written in a vacuum. I am grateful to CavanKerry Books for giving my book a home, and to those who have helped shape it: Lavina Blossom, Charlotte Davidson, Judy Kronenfeld, Eric Schwitzgebel, and my editor Baron Wormser, who all gave careful feedback on some or all of the poems. I also want to thank Dr. Zekos and Dr. Saste, my mother's and Marion's doctors, for taking the best care of them possible, and my own Dr. Simental, whose sense of humor and warmth make seeing the doctor almost fun. Lastly, I owe everything to my family: Ray, Kath, Heather, Jacob, Bradley, and especially my husband Lloyd, the most patient patient advocate around.

CavanKerry's Mission

CavanKerry Press is committed to expanding the reach of poetry to a general readership by publishing poets whose works explore the emotional and psychological landscapes of everyday life.

Other Books in the LaurelBooks Series

The Body at a Loss has been set in Myriad Pro, a humanist sans-serif typeface designed by Robert Slimbach and Carol Twombly for Adobe Systems in 1992. It is probably best known for its usage by Apple Inc., replacing Apple Garamond as Apple's corporate font from 2002 to around 2017.